The Family Constitution:

Agreements to Secure and Perpetuate Your Family and Your Business

Daniela Montemerlo Ph.D. and
John L. Ward, Ph.D.

Family Business Leadership Series, No. 20

Family Enterprise Publishers
P.O. Box 4356
Marietta, GA 30061-4356
800-551-0633
www.efamilybusiness.com

ISSN: 1071-5010
ISBN: 1-891652-15-X
© 2005
Third Printing

Family Business Leadership Series

We believe that family businesses are special, not only to the families that own and manage them but to our society and to the private enterprise system. Having worked and interacted with hundreds of family enterprises in the past twenty years, we offer the insights of that experience and the collected wisdom of the world's best and most successful family firms.

This volume is a part of a series offering practical guidance for family businesses seeking to manage the special challenges and opportunities confronting them.

To order additional copies, contact:
Family Enterprise Publishers
1220-B Kennestone Circle
Marietta, Georgia 30066
Tel: 1-800-551-0633
Web Site: www.efamilybusiness.com

Quantity discounts are available.

Other volumes in the series include:

Contents

Appendices

Exhibits

To Tina, my mother.

To my family.

Foreword

The two most effective practices implemented to protect and preserve the family business are 1) to build an independent board to strengthen the business and 2) to draft a Family Agreement to strengthen the family. This book is about the latter: the Family Agreement. *A Family Agreement is any kind of written principles and/or rules that regulate the relationship of the family with its business.*

While adoption of Family Agreements is becoming more and more popular for families committed to family and business continuity, the tradition of Family Agreements dates back centuries. The Mitsui family, one of the oldest entrepreneurial families in Japan, which still controls 20 percent of car manufacture and 15 percent of clothing production, wrote a constitution before 1800. The Muillez family of France, today a worldwide retailer, has a constitution that goes back more than one hundred years. Both families now have several hundred family owners who have clear guidelines for shared understanding of the ethics and rules of the family.

The *2002 Survey of American Family Businesses* states that 35 percent of business-owning families have some form of Family Agreement. According to recent research at Bocconi University, some form of Family Agreement is present in about one-third of Italian small and midsize enterprises. AIdAF (Associazione Italiana delle Aziende Familiari) and IEF (Instituto de la Empresa Familiar) — the Italian and Spanish family business associations, estimate that 10 and 12 percent, respectively, of their members have a comprehensive, formal Family Agreement and that the number is rising. In a recent analysis of family firms attending IMD business school's "Leading the Family Business" program (Lausanne, Switzerland) for large, global family firms, about 50 percent now report having a Family Agreement covering many areas.

The Family Business Consulting Group International has helped more than eighty families to develop Family Agreements over the past ten years. This book shares those experiences: Why have a Family Agreement? What should the contents include? How do you develop a Family Agreement? How is the agreement sustained over generations? What obstacles can stand in the way of a successful Family Agreement?

We designed this book to be useful to those families who are starting down the path toward a Family Agreement, for those who are trying to decide whether to begin or not and for those families who already have a Family Agreement and feel it is time to reassess it. This book will also help those families who have tried to write a Family Agreement in the past but for whatever reason have not finished the work.

The Family Constitution: Agreements to Secure and Perpetuate Your Family and Your Business is divided into two parts. The first provides an overview of the topic. Chapter 1 illustrates fundamental components of Family Agreements, while Chapter 2 analyzes the factors that can shape them.

The second part of the book delves into the agreement's components and offers detailed information and examples to help readers develop their own documents.

We would like to acknowledge many people for their assistance during our journey. A special thank you goes to our family business clients. We thank them for the privilege of being exposed to the most enriching and fascinating experiences both on the human and on the professional sides of life.

To our colleagues and friends of the Family Business Consulting Group International, we are grateful to all of you for the unique learning opportunity that this network has represented since its creation in 2000. We appreciate that you generously share with us your time, knowledge, practices and materials. We especially thank Miguel Angel Gallo and Guido Corbetta for their friendship, for the work we have been doing together for years and for their endless intellectual challenges.

We thank those who have helped this book become a reality. Craig Aronoff of The Family Business Consulting Group, Inc.®, Jane Aronoff of Family Enterprise Publishers® and Patricia Butler patiently and smartly accompanied us through the editing process. We thank you all for your help and support. Finally, it is understood that all mistakes that the book may contain are the authors' exclusive responsibility.

Daniela Montemerlo and John Ward
December 2004

Part I
The Family Agreement: An Overview

I: The Fundamental Components of a Family Agreement

The second generation of the Cordetto family in Argentina was considering the future for the eight cousins of the third generation. Several questions were making demands on people's time and energy:

- What are the rules for next-generation family members to work in the business?

- Is the family committed to next-generation business involvement and ownership, and if so, why?

- How does the family make decisions?

- How can the family educate themselves to address these subjects?

- Who should participate in the educational process and decision making?

- Is it more important to rely on the family's values and past experiences? Or is it better to set clear rules?

- If family members are expected to pursue higher education and outside work experience, can we still expect them to start at the bottom of the company as past generations have done?

- Will we need different compensation systems than in the past?

- How do we keep family shareholders who are not working in the business involved?

- What if a family member wants to sell his/her shares? Our corporate bylaws, have not been reviewed since the business began. How do we proceed?

A Family Agreement addresses these questions and many more.

Purpose

More and more business-owning families are working to adopt Family Agreements for several reasons:

- To keep family ownership united and to forge a broad and strong owning family's commitment to the future of the family's business.

- To give the family business a strong foundation and to build the confidence of non-family managers and business partners.

- To shape next-generation expectations for their roles in the business and as future owners.

- To keep the family together, preventing conflicts over unnecessary misunderstandings.

Content

Family Agreements can be as short as a one-page description of the family's values and mission or as long as fifty pages of policies and contractual stipulations. The intention of any Family Agreement is, explicitly or implicitly, to guide the family through important, possibly even contentious, decisions into the future. To do so, some families rely more on *philosophy*, others lean on *principles* and many believe they benefit greatly from precise *policies*. It is also valuable to consider who the parties to the Family Agreement are. Is the agreement for all family members or only for those who are shareholders?

In other words, a Family Agreement should address the following issues:

- **How** to resolve specific family firm issues.

- **What** to consider as key elements when making present and future decisions.

- **Why** the family wishes to address future issues.

- **Who** is included in decision-making and whom the decisions affect.

- **When** to review and revise the agreements.

Presented in a different way, a Family Agreement might include the following components:

- Preamble or Introduction for the Parties Involved (Who?)

- Statement of Family Values and Beliefs (Why?)

- Outline of Family Business Principles (What?)

- Chapters on Policies That Govern Family and Business Relations (How?)

- Conclusion on the Method to Make Amendments (When?)

Consider the common but complex subject of business leadership succession. In the Family Agreement Introduction, there might be an exchange of letters between two generations of family acknowledging and respecting each other. Moreover, the Family Agreement might articulate values that will shape succession, such as trust in outsiders as possible non-family candidates and belief in the inherent capacity of family members to grow and to develop as leaders.

Translating those values regarding the topic of succession might provide the following family business principles:

2

"Only the best person for the business can be CEO."

"A business must have one leader (not co-CEOs)."

"The roles of CEO and chairman should be separate."

"Family should be groomed, if at all possible, for the chairman of the board position."

Going further, the family may specify the process and criteria for selecting the successor. For example, "The Family Council will nominate the chairman candidate(s) to the business's board of directors' nominating committee." or "The search for the successor CEO will involve only the board's independent directors and will include consideration of external and non-family management candidates by a search firm and organizational psychologist."

Family Agreements can be very different in form, content and even names...

Family Agreements can be very different in form, content and even names (they may be referred to as family charters, contracts, protocols, codes of conduct, statements, etc.). Given this variety, we find it useful to think of "types" of Family Agreements. Each has a distinctive focus and perspective.

- **Owners' Contract (Shareholders' Agreement)** — specifies the legal understandings among shareholders (i.e., buy–sell agreement, redemption process, dividend rights, etc.)

- **Family Business Protocol** — defines the formal policies of family interaction with the business (i.e., employment rules, clear direction as to who can speak to the news media, evaluation process of family members for promotion and professional development, etc.)

- **Family Statement** — offers a philosophical set of views of what is important to the family (i.e., values statement, family mission statement, etc.)

The Family Statement has as a primary focus: the welfare of the family as a family. The Family Business Protocol considers the interests of the business as an institution. The Owners' Contract (Shareholders' Agreement) protects the rights of owners. (See Exhibit 1.)

EXHIBIT 1 ███████████████████████████████

Perspective of Family Agreements

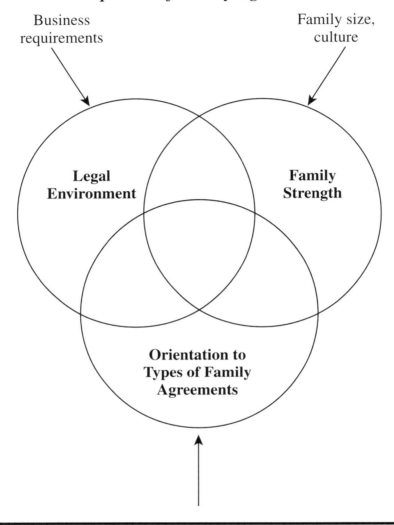

Business requirements

Family size, culture

Legal Environment

Family Strength

Orientation to Types of Family Agreements

Inherently, therefore, each type of Family Agreement takes a particular perspective — that of the family, the business or the ownership.

In fact, many successful long-lasting business-owning families consider each perspective in a balanced way. They attempt to articulate all elements of a Family Agreement in an integrated way — the Who (Preamble), the Why (Values and Mission), the What (Principles), the How (Policies and Contracts) and the When (Periodic Review and Revision). A Family Agreement that answers all the questions — who, why, what, how and when — is defined as a *Family Constitution,* the title of this book.

Process

The style and substance of Family Agreements varies, as it should, from culture to culture, country to country and family to family. Each family should adopt its own process for developing its Family Agreement and should address its issues with its own rules, depending on the nature of the business, the laws of the land and the culture of the family. This book will provide general approaches based on our experience and research. Our fundamental belief is that the process of forging a Family Agreement can be just as or more important than the content of the agreement itself. In fact, it is not difficult to develop abstract rules. It is far more difficult to make these rules fit within a family's particular situation.

...the process of forging a Family Agreement can be just as or more important than the content of the agreement itself.

The process of developing the Family Agreement builds family decision-making and problem-solving skills. The process educates family members about their own histories and their business as it functions today. The process motivates family members to consider the collective good and an overarching sense of purpose for business ownership and for family as family.

A successful Family Agreement is much more than a piece of paper; it is, instead, "paper in action." The process, which led to signing the agreement, strengthens trust and unity. The process becomes a means by which the family business may be elevated for change — providing new structures, new behaviors and new roles. The process, most importantly, fosters family commitment to personal and collective growth.

Conclusion

Family Agreements address the interest of the business with a clarity that invigorates the commitment of management and stakeholders. The agreement provides the vision that strengthens the resolve and devotion of ownership. The process of developing a Family Agreement builds family confidence and comfort.

The type of Family Agreement a business-owning family favors will affect not only the content of the agreement but also the process. We will discuss this further in Chapters 4 and 5. Which type of Family Agreement a family has also reflects certain fundamental assumptions about business and family, as will be discussed in Chapter 6. Over time, there is a natural gravity for all families — regardless of the agreement they start with — toward a full, formal Family Constitution.

From whatever perspective — family, business or ownership — as the family commences the process of developing its agreement education and confidence grow over time. Many families are motivated to ongoing efforts to develop more balanced and comprehensive Family Agreements — ultimately creating a Family Constitution. Enthusiasm and energy often grow along with the experience.

The Family Constitution, a comprehensive articulation of philosophy, principles and policies for the future that balances and synthesizes the welfare of family, owners and the business, is among the most important steps a business-owning family can take to secure and strengthen its business and, most preciously, its family.

II: What Shapes the Family Agreement?

Every Family Agreement is — or should be — unique, reflecting the distinct character and culture of the particular business-owning family, the nature of its business and applicable laws. This chapter explores those factors, focusing especially on the influence of the family's culture.

National laws and customs influence the content of Family Agreements. Owners' Contracts, of course, must conform to applicable law. Some countries' laws permit different classes of equity shares, restrict company share redemptions or allow a company's shares to be controlled through tax-advantaged foundations or trusts.

In addition, legal custom in different countries may encourage writing much of the Family Agreement as a contract or as a formal amendment to the corporate charter. If so, the agreement would likely become more specific and less flexible.

The company's strategic context also matters. In some countries, corporate debt is cheap, and in others, debt may be unavailable. Industry differences influence the Family Agreement. If the industry is rapidly growing and capital intensive, the dividend policy likely will be affected. If the family business is a highly skilled professional service firm, it is likely to have more rigorous employment policies for family members. Such a firm will also be more likely to restrict ownership to employed family members and possibly be more likely to offer ownership to non-family executives. When ownership includes non-family, governance rules may be quite different. A diversified business may have more and different roles for the family in the company's governance. It may also allow for different kinds of family goals or educational policies. (For more on how the business environment influences the family's policies, goals and roles, see *Strategic Planning for the Family Business*.) Certainly, the size of the firm and the liquidity it might provide are basic to the family's relationship to the firm.

Because the legal and strategic contexts are important, families typically include professional advisors and company executives or directors in the process of developing their Family Agreements. Lawyers and accountants explain the options and constraints. Board members constructively enter into the early stages of the development process to foster a dialogue on how family choices may affect the strength or direction of the business and vice versa.

Family Influences

The size of the family, mixed with the size of the business, fundamentally affects the content of the Family Agreement. Large families will likely have more family members not employed by the business than in the business. In such situations, the meaning, mission and values of the company have critical importance. The larger the family, the more likely the Family Agreement will stress the family purpose and philosophy. Generally speaking, the larger the business, the more flexible the rules of the Family Agreement will be. In fact, if the business has ample resources, it can absorb family evolution and change more readily. Consider the following exhibit:

EXHIBIT 2

The Influence of Family and Business Size

		Business Size	
		Small	**Large**
Family Size	Small	Business Focused and Rigid Rules	Business Focused and Flexible Rules
	Large	Family Focused and Rigid Rules	Family Focused and Flexible Rules

Exhibit 2 identifies two of several ways in which Family Agreements may differ: flexible versus rigid rules and family or business focused. There are several other common dimensions of difference in Family Agreements:

- Some Family Agreements are brief; others are very detailed.

- Some Family Agreements are enforced through moral authority; others, through legal authority.

- Some Family Agreements embrace ongoing family interactive processes (i.e., education, values affirmation, dialogue with the board of directors) to sustain family commitment and cohesiveness; others depend on their written document to constrain conflict.

All these variations seem to come from a specific cultural mentality of the owning family. Does the family feel it is *Business First* in its care and consideration? Alternatively, is it more *Family First*?

This difference in a family's orientation — Business First or Family First — shapes the content of the Family Agreement, ultimately the type of Family Agreement and even the process by which it is drafted, as you will note in the following exhibit.

A family's orientation — Business First or Family First — shapes the content of the Family Agreement.

8

EXHIBIT 3 ▆▆▆▆▆▆▆▆▆▆▆▆▆▆▆▆▆▆▆▆▆▆▆▆▆▆▆▆

Owning Family's Orientation

Family First	Business First
• Family Focused Meaning	• Ownership & Company Focused Meaning
• Flexible Rules	• Rigid Rules
• Brief	• Detailed
• Moral Authority for Enforcement	• Legal Authority for Enforcement
• Process Rich	• Content Complete

A *Family First* family will likely develop its Family Agreement more slowly, with more meetings, and include a family business consultant for facilitation. A *Business First* family will likely develop its Family Agreement more quickly, as a formal project, and likely depend more on its lawyer or accountant for advice.

The *Family First* or *Business First* orientation of the family strongly influences the very type of Family Agreement developed:

EXHIBIT 4 ▆▆▆▆▆▆▆▆▆▆▆▆▆▆▆▆▆▆▆▆▆▆▆▆▆▆▆▆

Owning Family's Orientation and Family Agreement's Type

Family First	Business First
Family Statement or Family Constitution	Owners' Contract or Family Business Protocol

Accordingly, it is valuable to explore how and why different families are different in terms of their priorities.

Family First versus Business First

Families, especially as they develop their Family Agreements, have various assumptions underlying the type and content and style of their Family

Agreements. They have basic assumptions as to what it takes to be a successful, long-lasting business. One such assumption relates to the desirability for innovation and entrepreneurship versus the appreciation of stability and consistency. Another assumption is the belief as to whether ownership and management need to be one, or whether separation is possible. Yet another assumption concerns the development of business leadership: must it come from within the family, or is it best if it does not? Finally, does an organization need one clear leader, or is it acceptable to have a leadership team, with sibling or cousin co-leaders?

Families also have basic assumptions about how families behave. Some feel conflict or at least separation is inevitable. Others feel owning a business brings family closer together. Some believe family closeness suffocates individuality. Others believe family closeness facilitates individual creativity and personal risk taking.

Families have basic assumptions about human nature as well. Some design their Family Agreements around the belief that wealth destroys human motivation and happiness. Others believe non-paid work (i.e., philanthropy and personal growth and achievement) can be as rewarding and of as much value as paid work.

The assumptions about family, business and human nature are reflected in two overarching perspectives:

1. The business is good for the family; or the business will risk the family's harmony.

Those who believe the business is good for the family argue that were it not for the business, the family would not be close, perhaps eventually fragmenting and ceasing to be a family that even sees each other. The business creates shared interests and provides a reason to bring the family together in creating an environment where all can work hard at strengthening family relationships.

Those who feel the business is a severe risk to the family argue that the requirements and resources of the business inevitably cause family conflict, bringing out the worst in family members — greed, selfishness and rivalry. If it weren't for the demands of the business, they reason, the family would be happier and closer.

2. The family is good for the business; or the family will harm the business's success.

Those who believe the family is good for the business cite the benefits of stable, caring ownership. They talk of the family's interest and commitment to the long term and to "doing the right thing." They see the family's values bringing special strengths to the business's culture.

Others fear family management competence is inevitably diluted, that family size and demands for money will sap the business and that family conflict will distract or divide the business. The long-held dreams of building a business that becomes a permanent memorial to the founder and a protected institution serving the community and employees are seen as threatened by family involvement.

Families, who feel conflicted on this score, believing that both the family and the business threaten each other, become concerned about protecting and preserving ownership security or personal financial security. These families are most likely on the path to selling the business.

Families, who see a positive, mutual, interdependent benefit, with the family enhancing the business and the business enhancing the family, seek to balance both perspectives — searching for the synergies between family and business. In fact, ownership concerns may be minimized. If ownership concerns are low, then the Family Agreement can be more flexible and adaptive.

These contrasting and various perspectives are summarized below. For each combination of perspectives, the fundamental goal of the Family Agreement is noted, plus the orientation to address *Family First*, *Ownership First* or *Business First*.

EXHIBIT 5

Perspectives About Family Business Ownership

	Business Ownership is Threat to the Family	Business Ownership is Opportunity for the Family
Family Ownership is Threat to the Business	Assure Financial Liquidity (Ownership First)	Protect Business (Business First)
Family Ownership is Opportunity for the Business	Protect Family (Family First)	Promote Family and Business Synergy (Balance)

Before applying these perspectives and orientations to the type of Family Agreement, it may be useful to consider where these perspectives originate.

Experience suggests the family's own history determines the family's ownership perspective. The family may have learned that the business created shared interests or, contrarily, that previous generations had been torn apart by family business arguments. Frequently it is a fabricated perspective forged by a controlling founder who wants to save the business as his or her personal legacy, even at the risk of disempowering or alienating his or her own family. Whatever the origin, **the perspective on the interaction of business and family and the corresponding orientation is the primary driver of the type, content and style of the Family Agreement, as well as the process by which it is developed as discussed in the next section.**

Type of Family Agreement

In fact, the family's assumptions on their business, family and human nature, plus the family's historical perspective on the interaction of family harmony and

11

The Family Constitution accepts that both the "Family First" and the "Business First" orientation need to be considered and balanced.

business ownership powerfully shape the choice of what type of Family Agreement to develop — Owners' Contract, Family Business Protocol, Family Statement or Family Constitution-and the choice of the process. A *Business First* bias will typically lead to a business executive, senior-generation, management-oriented drafting or review process resulting in a policy-based protocol. A *Family First* bias will likely lead to a family-led, inclusive and more democratic process and eventually to a Family Statement comprised of values and principles.

The Family Constitution includes all types of Family Agreements. The Family Constitution accepts that both the "Family First" and the "Business First" orientation need to be considered and balanced. The work behind developing a comprehensive Family Constitution means that the differing perspectives of family and business are synthesized. Therefore, the likely type of Family Agreement desired by a family greatly depends on these perspectives as shown in Exhibit 6.

EXHIBIT 6

Type of Family Agreement Desired

	Business Threat to Family	**Business Opportunity to Family**
Family Threat to Business	Owners' Contract (Shareholders' Agreement)	Family Business Protocol
Family Opportunity to Business	Family Statement	Family Constitution

Conclusion

In summary, the types of Family Agreements are determined by the variables sketched out in the following figure, with a special role for culture:

12

An Overview of Variables That May Shape a Family Agreement

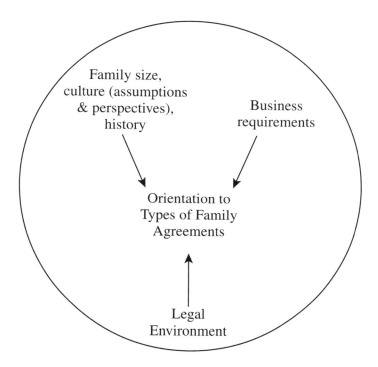

The type of Family Agreement usually evolves with the family's experience. More often, it usually evolves toward a Family Constitution. The business-owning family learns that more business formality is needed over time and that more emotional strength and commitment from the family are required.

In this evolution process, Family Statements are enhanced with more formal family conflict resolution processes and ownership governance systems. Family Business Protocols are enhanced with more reason to sacrifice and to work for the best interests of the family and its business. Owners' Contracts are completed by family and business philosophy, principles and policies, involving the family to a greater degree than fixing legal issues. Increasingly the family builds into its agreements amendability and adaptability. What is certain about the future is that the family and the business will change. Adaptability is, perhaps, the most important feature of a successful family business and business family.

Part II
Developing Your Own Agreement

III: Purposes of Family Agreements

There are several reasons why a business-owning family may forge a Family Agreement. Consider the three main perspectives and the related general purposes for a family to develop such an agreement:

- To foster the company's successful development.

- To maintain ownership unity and commitment.

- To reinforce family strength as family.

EXHIBIT 7

General Purposes of a Family Agreement

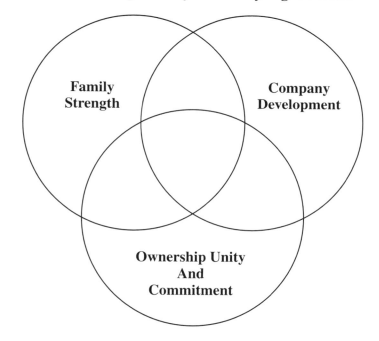

Family Strength

Company Development

Ownership Unity And Commitment

Company Development

From the company's perspective, some owning families begin working on a Family Agreement to manage a leadership succession process that cannot be postponed. Others want to prepare for succession well in advance, deciding entry

The Company Perspective

The Lopez family was composed of three branches. Second-generation members of each branch were serving on the board of directors, and they had children working in the business. For years, they had not undertaken any particular training and career path, until the president (a second-generation representative) and the CEO (a non–family member) announced their intention to step down within five years. At that point, the second generation realized the need to agree upon how the next president and/or CEO would be selected and how third-generation family members would have to prepare in order to be considered as candidates.

The O'Brian family had thirty-five heirs in the fourth generation, and the eldest were nearing the end of high school. The third generation decided it was time to decide common rules for the children's entry, compensation and career development in the family firm.

The Dorcäk family CEO felt the company was experiencing strategic challenges that made a stronger organization necessary. In particular, he felt the need to introduce Management by Objectives systems for both family and non-family managers, initiate managing committees and make compensation and career systems more appealing to outside managers. He proposed sharing with the family the principles and policies behind his proposed changes, which would affect eight family employees from the five family branches participating in ownership.

The Bellini family had decided to step down from all managing positions, delegating them to non-family executives. The board of directors needed to articulate clear performance standards to clarify owners' expectations and by which management would be held accountable.

The Elston family executives increasingly realized that a board composed only of themselves was inadequate. To cope with the future, they believed they would need a governance system that enabled them to get outside input and, perhaps, to go public in a few years. They thought it was necessary for the owning family to develop new rules for board composition and functioning.

and career criteria for the next generation that is not yet involved in the business. Some owning families intend to set the conditions for employing professional management or to guarantee the company a suitable governance system.

Ownership Commitment

If we take the point of view of ownership, there are also many specific reasons behind a Family Agreement. A common purpose is to set up rules (or change existing ones) to transfer shares in and outside the family and, particularly, to make sure that outside partners will be accepted only under certain conditions, assuring family control. Another purpose is to create a sort of internal market and/or agreement on dividend policies to meet shareholders' liquidity needs.

Sometimes owning families need to clarify their understanding as to what information is to be provided to shareholders, strengthening communication and building trust between managing and non-managing shareholders. A Family Agreement can also establish rules that define representation in governance bodies, protect minority shareholders' interests and safeguard family control. A Family Agreement can enable family owners to share the values and behaviors of

---

The Ownership Perspective

An old Italian company was controlled by twenty-five family shareholders. In the last three years, due to the unexpected death of two shareholders from the senior (fifth) generation and to other intrafamily transfers, the number of shareholders exploded from six to twenty-five. Five family shareholders worked in the company, and fourteen of the non-active twenty shareholders had little understanding of business. The company president realized the need to clarify the rights and duties of shareholders and to share rules to protect the company in case some wished to sell their shares. For their part, the new family owners wanted to be guaranteed adequate information in shareholders' meetings and proper representation on the board of directors. This required both the shareholders and the board to adopt new systems for nomination and functioning.

A Portuguese family ownership was composed of six shareholders (two founders and four children), none of whom held a majority. They had three companies and operated in different industries: wine, real estate and tourism. With three managing owners leading different businesses and ownership becoming more fragmented in the next generation, the family agreed to create a family holding company that controlled the three operating units, and to assign the three subsidiary presidents higher equity stakes in the companies they managed.

responsible ownership in current and future generations. Perhaps most important, it can state specific processes for solving ownership conflicts. Some examples are discussed in the following pages.

Family Strength

Families may want to draft a Family Agreement to reinforce shared values and to set up conditions for family members to act together, independent from their involvement

Family Agreements delineate a family's responsibility to its business.

in the business. A Family Agreement can also be aimed at providing financial and personal services for the family as a whole and its individuals or for sharing family assets. Some families provide for next-generation higher education while others establish emergency funds for family members in need.

Family Agreements delineate a family's responsibility to its business. Family Agreements provide powerful means to groom future owners and spell out the policies that relate family interests and business interests (i.e., family employment, marriage contracts, funding family events), providing a crucial reference point for the next generation.

The Family Perspective

A midsize company from California was composed of six members of the second generation, who were also shareholders of their agricultural business, and twenty members of the third generation, none of whom yet held any shares. Six family members were actively involved in the business: the president from the second generation and five from the third generation.

The president had always been supported by his brothers and sisters but was concerned about the next generation. Assuring shared values might be problematic. The company would not be able to provide employment for all shareholders.

Third-generation family members not involved in the business were very interested in becoming shareholders and to contribute both to the company (as non-employed owners) as well as to the family. Some had been asking themselves if their children would have any opportunity to have a career in the company. They enthusiastically accepted an invitation to a series of family meetings, with an agenda including developing principles and rules about such issues as how to keep family values alive, safeguarding previous generations' heritage; how to organize the family, both to support the business and also to help everyone find his or her own way; what to require for employment in the business; and how to prepare for the rights and duties of shareholders.

EXHIBIT 8 ▮▮▮▮▮▮▮▮▮▮▮▮▮▮▮▮▮▮▮▮▮▮▮▮▮▮▮▮▮▮▮▮▮▮▮▮

Purposes for a Family Agreement

GENERAL PURPOSES	SPECIFIC EXAMPLES
• To foster the company's successful development	– to manage a succession process – to prepare for succession – to set the conditions for professional management – to guarantee the company a suitable governance system
• To maintain ownership unity and commitment	– to set up rules to transfer shares in and outside the family – to create an internal market for family controlled shares and establish dividend policies – to set up proper shareholder understandings on information and representation – to share values and behaviors of responsible ownership – to state how to solve ownership conflicts
• To reinforce the strength of the family	– to keep a common patrimony of values – to set up conditions for family members to get together – to offer services for the family as a whole and for individuals in the family – to groom future owners in a responsible way – to delineate the family's responsibility towards the business

The Initiation of a Family Agreement

Families most often realize their need for a Family Agreement when they recognize the complexity of family business ownership. Usually the purpose and focus of the Family Agreement depends on which part of the family business system is becoming most complex — company, ownership or family. The most frequent complexities are described in Exhibit 9.

EXHIBIT 9

Complexity Factors that Trigger Family Agreements

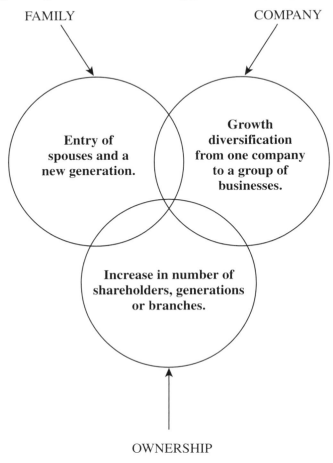

FAMILY   COMPANY

Entry of spouses and a new generation.

Growth diversification from one company to a group of businesses.

Increase in number of shareholders, generations or branches.

OWNERSHIP

Complexity needs to be managed proactively. In fact, recognition of future complexity and consequent development of a Family Agreement help generate possible solutions, promote discussion within the family and facilitate making decisions long before trouble occurs. Acting sooner rather than later also gives the family the ability to test the decisions agreed upon and to "fine-tune" them as necessary.

When problems arise and the owning family has not prepared, solutions must be found under conditions of greater time pressure, less flexibility and less objectivity. The temptation may arise to just "put on a bandage," without thinking of the precedent that this might create. The potential for painful — or even disastrous — conflict is much greater. In one second-generation French business-own-

Knowing one's history is crucial to preparing for the future.

ing family, the decision to share criteria for next-generation entry into the business was postponed a number of times. All agreed that recruiting family members would always respond to company needs but disagreed on other issues. One day a family manager decided to hire his son without telling anybody. The son had just left school and needed something to do. After a long and difficult discussion among family members in the business, the assignment was made into a temporary consulting job. Finding this agreement after the episode took a great deal of time and energy and didn't fully address the issue. The main danger that had to be faced was represented by next-generation potential employees for whom a critical precedent would have been set.

Managing complexity requires a systemic view of family business issues. "Just" acting on company, family or ownership might not be enough, as the three variables are interrelated. For instance, as the family grows, ownership may be spread among more people; in turn, extended ownership can affect company expansion or diversification. A proactive attitude is fundamental to anticipate the evolution of a family company in all its facets and all its dimensions as happened to a Massachusetts family. This family needed rules for the next generation. They also needed to clarify roles of family and non-family executives, as the company was expanding its product range and geographical markets. Finally, they needed a holding structure to strengthen family control and to create a shared voice among a very fragmented family ownership.

The need to deal with complexity is not the only factor that may induce a family's efforts. A family's history or family tension can also stimulate the Family Agreement process.

History, particularly past conflicts, can exert a major influence on the purpose, timing and type of Family Agreement. If litigation has occurred among owners, those who remained in the business will likely be inclined to develop Owners' Contracts (Shareholders' Agreements) to cope with extended ownership in the next generation. Families divided by personal conflicts will tend to devote time and energy to have next-generation members know each other and develop a common culture. Companies where incompetent family members caused business problems will likely be protected by strict rules for entry and career development in the next generation.

Knowing one's history is crucial to preparing for the future. However, a family must not be paralyzed by problems of the past. Nor should a family assume that past successful practice will be adequate to deal with the future's challenges.

In the Lopez family, the president took a long time to develop methods of communicating with shareholders and on relations between shareholders and the board. He had a hard time realizing the importance of these issues, as he had become accustomed to his siblings' trust in managing the company. When his nephews and nieces rejected his nomination process to replace two board members, it was quite a shock, and it made him aware that times had changed.

Conclusion

A Family Agreement is undertaken for different purposes — family, ownership or business reasons. Families orient themselves towards a certain purpose at certain times depending on their evaluation of present and future complexity, the influence that their history exerts on them and even on current family tensions. **Learning from and respecting the past while acting proactively in the present will improve the chance that the agreement will move the family business toward a successful future.**

There are problems that a Family Agreement will not solve. A Family Agreement is not the way to address or heal long-standing family disputes or emotional wounds. Instead, seek counselling to resolve those issues. Drafting of a Family Agreement then can be a process that will test the strength of the family's resolve to move forward together.

Families without family businesses might, but rarely do, draft statements of family mission, values and policies for mutual support and future harmony. Families in business together have the more obvious impetus to collectively envision and prepare for their future. That is among the blessings of owning businesses as families.

IV: The Contents of Family Agreements

Chapter 1 introduced the basic sections that can be found in a Family Agreement: the preamble (who?); family values and beliefs (why?); family business principles (what?); family business policies that govern family and business relations (how?); and the process to review and revise the agreement (when?). This chapter delves more deeply into each section, analyzes the content possibilities and provides examples.

The Preamble

A Family Agreement generally begins with a preamble that outlines the agreement's fundamentals. The preamble presents the family and the company, explains the reasons why the family forged the agreement, introduces the types of regulations agreed upon and describes anticipated benefits.

Specifically, the following points are common in the preamble:

- The purposes of the agreement (see Chapter 3).

- The subject of the agreement — what's covered (i.e., business, holding company, family office).

- The content — what's included.

- The parties to the agreement — who signs it.

- The power of the agreement — enforcement philosophy .

Sometimes, the agreement's preamble is enriched by a short history of the family and/or the company. The agreement may also document special commitments made by different generations to help assure the success of the agreement. For instance, the senior generation might state that it will engage in facilitating leadership succession; the next generation, in its part, might commit or guarantee security, certain rights or assets to the senior generation.

Consider the example that follows:

EXHIBIT 10 ■■

Selections from a Family Business Protocol

Foreword

To date, our company has been governed according to an implicit agreement among members of the first generation. Due to ownership's coming fragmentation and the company's continuing growth, it has become critical to share principles and rules for the family-firm relationship and to make them explicit, to preserve the company's viability and the owners' unity.

Purposes of the agreement

- to share, and make explicit, that family and firms are different types of organizations both in terms of their goals and their functioning rules;

- to share principles of family-firm relationship and make them explicit;

- to share the rules that derive from these principles;

- to give the family firm a governance system that be suitable to its present and future structure;

- to engage all those who sign the protocol and, by this means, commit them to it both morally and legally;

- to penalize incorrect behaviors.

Object of the family protocol: To define and govern the relationship between our family and all the companies it may control, both directly and indirectly, for the whole period of the protocol's validity.

Signatures of the family protocol: The agreement is signed by all family shareholders (first and second generation). Signing the Agreement is a necessary condition to becoming a "family shareholder," and for admission to the family shareholders' meeting.

Family Values and Beliefs

In addition to the preamble, Family Agreements generally present the core values and beliefs of the family. That is, families explicitly acknowledge the shared values and beliefs behind the principles and/or policies they have developed. (For additional information on this topic see *Valores corporativos y empresas familiars* and *The Role of Family in Family Business*.)

Such values and beliefs may refer to both present and future. They state what matters to the family, its culture, its mission and what the family wants to become — its vision for future generations. The values and beliefs focus on the family strictly as a family or also may apply to the assets and operating companies owned by the family. Families sometimes choose labels such as the following:

- **Family's guiding beliefs as family** — the values that the family shares and practices in individual behaviors; at work; in relations among family members; in relation to the outside world; and with regard to family wealth. Examples of values are discretion, discipline, common identity, unity and commitment to the company.

- **Family's guiding beliefs as a family business** — the company's entrepreneurial vocation; its competitive goals within its industry; its economic goals; its role in society; its organizational philosophy; and its leadership style. Some examples include social responsibility, industry leadership, competitiveness, profitability, commitment to excellence, innovation, transparency and accountability, and meritocracy.

- **Family's ownership vision** — the present family owners' beliefs on who should become the future owners (i.e., everybody, only those who will work in the company, both family and non-family shareholders); the owning family's commitment to the company's continuity; family members' contributions and expectations. Some examples are involvement, commitment, legacy and stewardship.

- **Family's business vision** — the kind of family business the family seeks; the possible roles of non–family and family members in the business; and company strategy and performance.

Other families also articulate the conditions for ceasing to be a business-owning family. Typically, this conclusion is based on the clear violation of its values and beliefs or a level of distrust among the ownership.

Exhibits 11 and 12 offer two examples of sections from Family Agreements that focus on values and beliefs.

EXHIBIT 11 ■■■■■■■■■■■■■■■■■■■■■■■■■■■■■■■■■

Family Values and Beliefs

Our commitment to trust will be the cornerstone of our strengths.

We will always strive to understand and fulfill the obligations of responsible family ownership.

Our beliefs will be the foundation for a growing, healthy enterprise that benefits all its constituents:

- A strong family with sound values creates a strong business with sound values. We value integrity, trust, commitment, personal growth and respect for individuals.

- A strong, effective family provides continuity in values to a business it owns.

- Continuity of values allows the business to take a long-term perspective that encourages learning, risk taking, innovation, entrepreneurialism and reliable partnerships.

- Family business ownership provides a common interest and a dynamic learning environment in which to build a strong, effective family.

- A successful family business creates benefits that result in freedom, opportunity and security for family members.

- Being responsible owners is an ongoing learning process that benefits family members of all ages.

- Family businesses are responsible to employees, business partners, the community at large, the private enterprise system, and past and future family generations.

- Family businesses that strive to be role models for other family businesses benefit society by sharing their learning with others and by supporting and promoting private enterprise.

- A strong family business adds value to society by creating change, promoting healthy competition, generating growth and exemplifying good citizenship.

EXHIBIT 12 ████████████████████████████

Family Values and Goals

The values that G2 leaves to G3:

- Sense of labor and responsibility;

- Unity, harmony, mutual understanding and love among family owners;

- Ethical behavior, inspired by discretion and honesty;

- Trust in company directors and managers;

- Attachment to the family business;

- Balance between work and family;

- Sense of shareholders' rights and duties.

As a family company, we want to have:

- Leadership in our country, among the best in Europe;

- Growth consistent with our competitors and our markets;

- Profitability higher than the industry average;

- Growth based on self-financing and financial caution – using outside equity only in extreme situations;

- Dividends that respect the company's needs, but are consistent with market levels;

- Complete information for shareholders;

- Opportunities of professional growth for family members.

Family Business Principles

Reading statements of family values, one might think, "Beautiful words, but where does this lead?" Assuming a family has declared a commitment to the company and a sense of ownership responsibility to be among its guiding beliefs, what's next to concretely foster company success? In other words, how does the family make its values concrete and accomplish the purposes of the Family Agreement?

The answer is the "what" of a Family Agreement, and it lies in family business principles. As stated in Chapter 1, principles represent the family's fundamental references when making present and future decisions. Continuing with the example above, a family's business principles might state that, given its deep attachment to the business, the family agrees that professional governance is essential; the board must be composed of top-level people; and the company must always follow the highest ethical standards. **Principles lay the groundwork for the tough decisions every business family must make.**

Generally speaking, family business principles concern the core issues of family–firm relationships, such as those below:

- Employment — entry, training, career development, compensation, assessment, rewards and sanctions, insurance, exit, leadership positions and their special requirements, dealing with family and non-family employees.

- Ownership — access to shares, share transfer, company evaluation, dividends, share distribution, resources for liquidation, transparency, shareholders' meetings structure

- Business governance — design of the governance system; access to the board; board responsibilities; board composition; relations between board, shareholders' council and top management.

Principles represent the family's fundamental references when making present and future decisions.

- Top management — managing committee composition, role and succession.

- Family governance — roles and composition of the family council and foundation, communication between family and business board, education and development for governance.

- Conduct inside and outside of the business — conflicts of interest, relations with the press and personal behavior.

- Agreement's amendability — the timing of review and the agreement's process for amending the document.

Sometimes family business principles make explicit reference to further regulations that are going to deal with the various issues in a more specific or detailed manner. These are the family business policies, also referred to as Family Business Protocol.

EXHIBIT 13 ▮▮▮▮▮▮▮▮▮▮▮▮▮▮▮▮▮▮▮▮▮▮▮▮▮▮▮▮▮▮▮▮▮▮▮

Family Business Principles Regarding a Board of Directors

The board of directors will be the maximum corporate governance body, responsible for increasing the company's value in the medium and long term. This responsibility will be carried on by:

- taking part in strategy formulation;

- mentoring development of the group's top management;

- assuring effective controls and accurate reporting.

Functioning rules will be contained in the Board of Directors charter, which will consider the following recommendations:

- Directors' appointment will respect the law and the articles of association norms. (In case a director has to represent various owners, the more capable owner will be appointed.);

- If convenient and possible, directors should not serve on the board more than two terms of 5 years each, and rotation among most capable family members ought to be promoted;

- Advisors can be appointed to assist the board;

- After succession, the directors' compensation will be calculated according to market criteria;

- Meetings will be held quarterly.

It is recommended that some members of the third generation take part in board meetings and represent the family whenever possible, provided that they are prepared to do so well, and that they do not prejudice the family business's image.

Family Business Policies

Some families create Family Agreements composed mainly of principles. However, other families take a further step, asking themselves, "Once we have decided upon a certain principle, how might it apply to a specific situation?" For example, a family may state the principle that the board of directors has to be a functioning one, which leads to the conclusion that the board must be composed of capable family directors, assisted by independent and highly skilled advisors. But how do we decide when family members are capable enough to be appointed to the board? What criteria are used? How old must the family member be, and what should the education and work experience be?

Family business policies represent the "how" of a Family Agreement. Based on principles, the family "translates" the principles into much more detailed rules. For more information, see *Developing Family Business Policies: Your Guide to the Future.*

In some cases, family business policies may be quite prescriptive but may rely on moral enforcement. In other cases, law determines the enforcement, and policies are formulated as if they were clauses of contracts or articles of association, depending, of course, on the issues under discussion and jurisdiction. If the issue emphasizes ownership or governance (i.e., transfers of shares, functioning of the shareholders' meeting, appointment of directors, voting outcomes for board decisions), the rules may have significant legal implications. Issues regarding next-generation employment, for example, might be considered either morally or legally binding. In any case, they should not be transferred into the company's bylaws.

In the next example, the family shared such guiding values as meritocracy, stewardship and commitment to the company's continuity, profitability and competitiveness. Based on such values, they shared the principle that all family members can be employed only if they are skilled enough to occupy management positions and add significant value to the family company. This principle was developed into the policies that follow.

EXHIBIT 14

A Family Business Policy for: Family Members' Entry into the Company

All young family members will have the opportunity to have an interview with expert consultants about their aptitudes for the purpose of professional career guidance, once they have completed their education. All young family members will be tutored by senior family members other than their parents.

eligible to work in the business, all young family members must meet wing meritocratic criteria:

- Undergraduate degree;

- Knowledge of a foreign language;

- Two years of experience outside the family business;

- Favorable support in the company by an expert in personnel recruiting and the Vice President of Human Resources.

Decisions will be made by the family holding board by a qualified majority (4/5). In all cases, young family members have to be hired according to the business's actual needs.

The family holding board will support the career development of young family members after they have entered the group.

For family members who are not hired, shareholders commit to help them as follows:

- Offer consulting relationships, based on the business's actual needs and at market conditions. After the initial period of two years, the professional relationship must evolve in such a way that such consulting does not represent more than 10% of the family member's earned income;

- Consider funding family members' entrepreneurial ventures;

- Provide career counsel every five years, as requested; and

- Be available to review past decisions with an open mind to consider new information if relevant.

Process to Review and Revise the Agreement

Amendability is appropriate either during the agreement's lifetime or when it expires (for example, every five years, according to Italian law). The best agreements have a certain flexibility and openness, as family and business circumstances will invariably change. The ability to adapt to changes is an essential and fundamental strength of healthy families. However, it is crucial to determine whether a proposed change fills a gap that has been created by a new situation or introduces inconsistency by responding to an individual's personal needs. Exhibit 15 offers an example of amendment rules.

EXHIBIT 15

How to Change the Agreement: The Guitar's Family Business Protocol

- The protocol will be changed with the favorable vote of the majority of the holding company's directors.

- The protocol's duration is ten years and the expiration date may not be postponed.

- If the holding company's board of directors unanimously agrees, a transition period can be admitted after the protocol's expiration during which a new protocol or updates to the present one will be formulated and the previous one will be temporarily valid.

At this point, we can summarize the four sections of a Family Agreement discussed so far and include possible topics for each section.

EXHIBIT 16

Contents of Family Agreements

BASIC SECTIONS	CONTENTS
• Introduction	• Purposes • Subject • Contents • Parties • Power
• Family Values and Beliefs	• Values as a family • Values as a family business • Vision as owners • Vision for the business
• Family Business Principles	• Employment • Ownership • Business governance • Top management • Family governance • Conduct in the business and outside • Agreement amendability
• Family Business Policies	• Employment • Ownership • Business governance • Top management • Family governance • Conduct in the business and outside • Agreement amendability (timing, majority votes, etc.)

Internal Consistency of Family Agreements' Contents

As discussed in Chapter 1, Family Agreements can feature various combinations of values, principles and policies. They can focus on a specific issue or encompass a variety of issues.

The agreement's contents must be internally consistent. At first glance, this sounds obvious. As shown in the previous examples, family values and beliefs should naturally drive family business principles, which in turn should drive family business policies. On the other hand, consistency is not automatic and has to be constantly monitored. Experience suggests that the risk of inconsistencies is particularly high when policies are first being developed or later amended. A level of risk also occurs when the principles behind the policies have not been thoroughly discussed.

When principles are explicit, consistency between principles and policies can be easily checked. In case of inconsistency, it is likely that the family may be "putting a bandage" on underlying problems and the principles behind policies might not be shared by all who are taking part in the agreement.

For instance, one family asked next-generation members to draft family business principles, and they came up with statements such as "merit compensation systems attract the best professionals and safeguard the company's economics." When it came to drafting policies, they proposed high compensation for all family members in management. This was based on their lifestyles rather than on their job responsibilities and performance. Discussion with the family's consultants highlighted the difficulty the group had grasping the concrete implications of principles.

Sometimes it is difficult for a family to state their principles explicitly. In some cases, families discovered that they cannot arrive at shared policies or the policies being proposed are inconsistent with their principles, because the family members' principles were assumed consistent with one another but actually were not. There cannot be consistency if the family has not truly searched for common principles. This search can be either fostered or confounded by the founders of the business. Founders, by nature, usually prefer ambiguity of principles and flexible policies and find it difficult to set concrete principles.

Amending a Family Agreement represents another important test of consistency within the contents of the agreement and between the agreement and the family business situation. Families might discover that some policies no longer represent the best application of their values and principles. A family may conclude that rules about entry into the company were so strict that they demotivated smart young people and threatened to leave no successors. Some principles may have become outdated, such as unwillingness to take on debt. Another possibility is that a family member might challenge the agreement, to solve a personal problem.

Conclusion

Family Agreements can include family values, family business principles, and business and ownership policies. Contents must be internally consistent, and consistency should be maintained over time.

V: It's the Process That Matters

We believe the *process* of developing the Family Agreement is more important than its contents. Our experience indicates that there are various types of Family Agreements with differing contents. A Family Agreement may or may not be successful. Chapter 7 will illustrate that most criteria for success are related to the process of developing the document, not to the document's philosophies, principles or policies. (For more insights on process, see *Family Protocols in Spain: A Survey on 10 Years of Experience*).

> *We believe the process of developing the Family Agreement is more important than its contents.*

The process for developing a Family Agreement will be described through five phases:

- Initiation

- Formulation

- Approval

- Implementation

- Review

In each phase, the participants in the process will be discussed, as well as the roles they play. In addition, the difficult issues that confront the development process will also be presented.

The Process Phases

As most business-owning families do not have a Family Agreement, we will take the process from its very inception to conclusion.

Initiation Phase. The process of developing a Family Agreement almost always starts informally. One or a few informal leaders in the family feel the need to foster family understanding, cohesiveness or agreement. Occasionally the process is initiated by an advisor to the family or a concerned non-family executive or director. The initiators typically seek to broaden sensitivity and support for the idea by first recommending education on the subject. Often a newspaper or magazine article about a family business in crisis is circulated. Books, seminars or visits to other business-owning families are common. These efforts help build a shared language and broader motivation.

Frequently those wanting to initiate the process are not the ones in positions of business or family power. Those in power may resist the initiative, as they are comfortable with the status quo. Effective initiators must plant the seeds and build a coalition of support by explaining different benefits of the effort, in order to arouse interest. Sensing how to introduce change is an important skill to begin the process.

Deciding who actually will be involved in creating the Family Agreement is often the most complicated decision in the initiation phase. For small families, involving everyone in a discussion is often the best approach. Yet whether "everyone" includes in-laws and at what age the next generation is eligible to participate need to be resolved. (See *Family Meetings: How to Build a Stronger Family and Stronger Business* for more on who from the family should participate.) In larger families, a committee and possibly subcommittees move the effort forward. In such cases, who's on the committee needs to be decided. Most often, asking for volunteers suffices. Generally, it is best to be inclusive rather than selective.

Who volunteers or who is selected is likely a result of what motivates the desires for the Family Agreement. If the Family Agreement is needed to address a problem, the various perspectives should be represented. If the Family Agreement is to prepare for the next generation, members from that generation need to be involved. If the purpose of the Family Agreement is to write an Owners' Contract (Shareholders' Agreement), then it is (mostly) shareholders who are involved, often in such a way as to represent different branches. If the intent of the Family Agreement is business protocol, then perhaps a non-family executive and/or independent director will be included, if not in formulation, at least to give advice on the validity of policies being developed.

If the family business has an active board that includes independent directors, whatever the type of agreement, it is wise to have the formulating committee periodically communicate with them. That helps keep up momentum and assures objectivity.

A coordinator or chair of the project will need to be selected from within the family. In some cases, co-chairs can be more effective. It's best if the business's CEO is not the leader of the process. The more family centered the process, the more likely to enhance the owning family's commitment.

A facilitator can be especially helpful in the process. If the focus of the agreement is an Owners' Contract (Shareholders' Agreement), the facilitator may be an attorney. If the agreement incorporates the Family Business Protocol, a family business consultant or advisor will be valuable both to facilitate and to lend expertise. Usually families find it difficult to facilitate themselves. An outside voice often assures broad and balanced contributions. There is also an acquired art to managing meetings. Consider these questions: Where to begin? How to organize the agenda? Whom to include? What to communicate throughout the process? These are often questions that a professional facilitator or outside advisor can help to answer.

Perhaps the greatest challenge in drafting a Family Agreement is how to lead the process when the family has never had a process before. Each decision, even those as basic as starting time or rules on smoking, must be preceded by developing agreed-upon methods to make decisions. Making these decisions is often awkward. A decision-making procedure should be established as early in the process as possible — preferably in the initiation stage.

Most small families (up to ten people) use consensus to make decisions. With this approach, if more than one person does not concur, the decision is reworked. Many large families set a substantial majority (i.e., 66 percent or 75 percent) as necessary to reach a conclusion. Sometimes the nature of the topic calls for different voting procedures, as will be discussed.

An initial and very critical task for most families is how to agree on the decision-making procedure before there is a decision-making procedure in place. These are the times when future family leadership often emerges.

Another early decision that requires a decision-making procedure before most families have one is how to select a facilitator and define their role. For a smaller family, selecting a facilitator by anything less than unanimous consensus is risky. The chosen facilitator should be acceptable to everyone even if he or she is not everyone's first choice. In other words, a veto power should be respected but used only by someone who has very strong objections. A facilitator who fails because a malcontent sabotages the process is a huge setback for all.

After deciding who will guide and participate in the process and how decisions will be made, the next steps are to determine what type of agreement is needed and to draft its table of contents. See the Appendices of this book as well as the previous and next chapters for examples.

Formulation Phase. The next challenging question in the development of a Family Agreement is whether this should be a process or a project. A process is slow and evolves while cultivating support. Each topic or issue is discussed in full at family meetings and/or shareholders' meetings. Understanding and support are nurtured along the way. Each topic may require multiple discussions before a sense of acceptance is achieved. Some in the family will greatly enjoy the dialogue, education and opportunity to be involved. Others will be frustrated by the inefficiency. Those speaking the most are often those who have been least involved in the past. A process-intensive approach can easily take two or three years to complete.

Others would prefer to see the effort as more of a project. A task force can do the homework and present the recommendation to the group as a whole. A project can be completed in a shorter time period. Indeed, an advisor or consultant could prepare a full first draft for consideration.

It is a difficult balancing act between process and project. The facilitator will work to blend both approaches and assign different roles to different people based on their personal styles and desires. Different techniques can be used, including small-group discussions, expert presentations or other activities to encourage fun as well as foster productivity. Each meeting is designed to assure some work is completed, some work is debated and new subjects are introduced. Documenting the progress and keeping each draft can provide valuable additions to the family's archives.

As previously mentioned, directors can be used for feedback. During the formulation phase it is often valuable for the family to report progress to its board of directors. In fact, the process facilitator should feel special accountability to the board. Though the owning family is responsible for the agreement, the board can help assess its application for the company. Early in formulation, the facilitator can be invited to a board meeting to outline the schedule and budget and to respond to questions. Periodically the facilitator should update progress in the process for the board. The board will help the family keep its momentum and help keep the facilitator on schedule. The board might also ask some questions that neither the family nor the facilitator considered. Advisors can be helpful as well, and particularly lawyers for legal expertise and assistance in the wording of the document.

Whether the agreement is completed quickly or slowly, it is important to always consider it as a work in progress. New issues and ideas constantly arise. Agreeing on an amendment process is a key decision to make at this stage in the process. After completion, it will be necessary to identify an ongoing review committee to address proposed amendments.

Approval Phase. Similar to deciding who should be involved before there is a process to make such decisions, how to ratify a document and set rules before the rules are established is also a potentially challenging conundrum. The approval process should be established early, preferably in the formulation phase, before contentious issues arise.

Voting to ratify the completed Family Agreement can take several forms: unanimity, consensus, super-majority or majority. Super-majority may be defined as 60, 67, 75 or 80 percent, depending upon the family. Making decisions by consensus, but not necessarily unanimously, is a special skill. Some families actually begin the whole Family Agreement development process with an educational session on consensual decision-making. A consensus does not require 100 percent agreement, but it does need 100 percent acceptance. Acceptance is earned by respecting each family member's views. However, if 90 percent support acceptance and the remainder feel well heard, we recommend that the minority "stand aside," respecting the conviction of the family as a whole.

Which ratification style is used for large families is often a matter of what aspects of the Family Agreement are being considered.

A discussion on the voting process raises a fundamental question: Should votes be based on per share or per person representation? Family Statements are usually voted on a per capita (per person) basis, often including those who may not yet own shares. Owners' Contracts (Shareholders' Agreements) are ratified on a per voting share basis. The Family Business Protocol is usually best considered on a per person basis, as in-laws and the next generation are particularly important to the implementation of the policies established. Some families, however, prefer that the Family Business Protocol be more like the Owners' Contract (Shareholders' Agreement) in its ratification.

Another consideration is whether there is an open vote or a secret ballot. Open ballots are encouraged, but for some families in some situations, secret ballots are desired. However, these questions are resolved, deciding who votes, how the votes are counted and how voting takes place should be determined early in the process.

EXHIBIT 17

Suggestions for Approving the Family Agreement

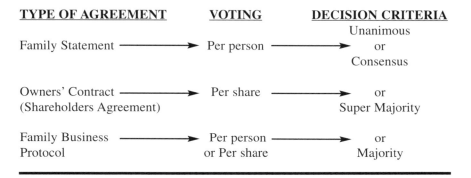

TYPE OF AGREEMENT	VOTING	DECISION CRITERIA
Family Statement ⟶	Per person ⟶	Unanimous or Consensus
Owners' Contract ⟶ (Shareholders Agreement)	Per share ⟶	or Super Majority
Family Business ⟶ Protocol	Per person or Per share ⟶	or Majority

If one member or one branch of the family is constantly vetoing ratification, that person or branch might prefer that their business ownership be bought out. Before such a thought is entertained, however, many families form a subcommittee to try to negotiate differences successfully. Even during the Family Agreement drafting process, all efforts are directed toward the priority of keeping the family together.

Typically, ratification is not a sophisticated political process. Indeed, it is most often a celebration. Attaching some ceremony to the signing of the document — perhaps even as each part is completed — can greatly enhance the process. The celebration is fun and reinforces both the documents and the family. For the young people in the family, attending such celebrations can be like a rite of passage. A copy of the agreement should be given to each family member for his or her safekeeping.

It is also valuable to communicate the completed works and the family ceremony to directors, key executives and advisors and others important to the family and business. Some families even announce the achievement in their employee newsletters. Some post the family's values and commitment in the company lobby and on their promotional material.

Implementation Phase. Without implementation, developing a Family Agreement is just an exercise. The emotional effort and energy that goes into the process of drafting the agreement is extraordinary. For most families, the process represents their most significant investment of vulnerability and openness. If nothing comes of the Family Agreement, the family will be reluctant to try again. Families can become very cynical toward future efforts.

Implementation has several dimensions:

- Execution of next steps — completing called-for revisions of corporate bylaws; drafting of legal agreements; adding new board members; setting up the family employment committee.

- Continued development of Family Agreement — writing additional policies or finishing incomplete ones to be included in the future.

- Establishment of new structures or processes — revising the board of directors; developing the family council; presenting an agreed-upon succession process to the board.

- Consistent application — assuring that established policies and rules are followed; making sure that exceptions are minimized and, if they occur, are explained.

The implementation phase is best measured against a plan that identifies the critical steps in the realization of the Family Agreement with specific dates of completion as defined early in the process. Families (and especially those members dependent on the business) are heartened and recommitted as implementation dates are achieved. All involved in the family business become anxious if implementation milestones and dates are missed. Failure to meet commitments may be seen as a lack of discipline, professionalism or commitment. As in all things, fulfilling commitments is important to trust — in this case, trust in the family and trust between the owning family and those responsible for the company.

One way to help assure implementation — or assist in an understanding of implementation shortfalls — is to create an objective forum for accountability. The company's board of directors could serve that role, as could the respected family or owners' council.

Review Phase. Implementation never really ends. Once the Family Agreement is completed, there are continuous revisions as the family regularly reviews the agreement and as generational transition proceeds. Some families review their agreements each year, while others work on three- to five-year cycles.

As we stated earlier, the Family Agreement needs a specific process by which it may be amended. Families may fine-tune the Family Statement portion of their agreement continuously as ongoing family meetings offer new insights into the family's values. Family Business Protocols are wisely reviewed after each challenging application, allowing the family to consider what was learned from experience and make revisions for the future. However, if Family Business Protocols are revised too often, they lose credibility and power.

Owners' Contracts (Shareholders' Agreements) are a special case. They are enforceable by law. The amendment procedures are in the agreement. A crucial part of the Owners' Contract is the termination or expiration date of the agreement. In many jurisdictions worldwide, the length of the contract is based upon the laws of the jurisdiction. Families often select a time to review and renew the contract. If the contract has a ten-year life, the family may choose to review it at five years in an attempt to extend it for ten more years. Doing so relieves pressure as the prescribed termination date approaches. At a minimum, **each generation should consider reviewing, revising and renewing the contract.**

Generally speaking, unanimity should not be required to amend or extend the contract. A small minority should not be allowed to paralyze the process. Supermajorities or, in any case, majorities that prevent single branches from blocking decisions are useful for renewing Owners' Contracts.

A summary of the five phases of the Family Agreement process, who is involved and the key tasks follows.

EXHIBIT 18 ▐

The Process of Developing and Managing the Family Agreement Process: An Overview

Phases	Participants	Main Activities
Initiation	Informal family leaders from the family or the business	Education on family agreements and family business "best practices"
	Eventually all family members	Education on family decision-making approaches
	Possibly a consultant or advisor	Definition of who participates, who leads and who facilitates the process
		Selection of consultant or facilitator
		Determination of how meeting decisions will be made
		Decision on type and table of contents, method of ratification and review committee
Formulation	Family members typically working through task force or committees or the Family Council or owners' council	Design of meetings: frequency and style
		First drafts
	Facilitators	Family and/or owners' meetings to discuss drafts

43

	Advisors to provide expert-ise and background	Reporting to business board of directors
	Company directors to test conclusions	Test of legalities with advisors
		Collection of meeting notes for family archives
		Agreement on method of ratification, review commit-tee and amendment process
Approval	All family members involved in approval	Negotiating team to resolve final differences of opinion
		Celebration ceremonies
		Announcements to key constituents
Implementation	Management and Board of company	Implementation plan
	Implementation task forces	Execution of next steps
	Board/owners' council/Family council assembly	Development of Agreement
		Introduction of new processes and structures
	Accountability forums	Application of principles and policies to everyday behavior
		Constant review
		Communication to key constituents
Review	Review committee	Reinforcement of family values
	All family members involved in amendments' approval	Policy revisions
		Contract revisions

The Role of Third Parties/Advisors

Different kinds of advisors can assist the Family Agreement process. The family's existing consultant may be used or a new one hired specifically to formulate the agreement. It can be a single person or a team of professionals with complementary competences (e.g., a family business consultant, a lawyer and an accountant, depending on the size and complexity of the family and the business). There are also cases in which outside directors or other business-owning families act as informal family advisors.

Advisors can act as educators, clarifying the Family Agreement's purposes, possible contents, rules of the game and any other relevant issues.

Advisors can play multiple roles in the process of developing a Family Agreement.

Advisors are in a unique position with respect to the family. They are outsiders and able to look at family firm issues from a detached perspective and act objectively. This enables them to act as process facilitators, helping family members to express their opinions and feelings on difficult issues, to listen to one another and to discuss issues calmly and constructively. Some advisors may be mediators and able to play a facilitating role. More frequently, they act both as facilitators and as experts of all relevant subjects (family business, business law, tax, strategic management).

Outside professionals are often asked to be the agreement's writers as well. This role can be interpreted in various ways. Sometimes advisors behave as coauthors, putting down in words the shared values, principles and policies that emerge from the family. In this role, they give their own opinions and proposals, but they ask the family to play a very active role. At other times, they act as the main authors, interviewing all family members, creating a text on their own, submitting it to the family, which plays a less participative role. This happens, typically, when the family is new to the topic and needs to produce an agreement quickly.

Under these circumstances, advisors may also play the role of project leaders. More frequently, as the family matures in its own experience, the professional's role is simply one of assistance to the company or family leaders.

Finally, advisors can act as educators, clarifying the Family Agreement's purposes, possible contents, rules of the game and any other relevant issues. This role can be particularly important not only at the beginning, but also in following phases, especially when the scheduled process evolves into an ongoing permanent one.

Defining the consultant's role is one of the most difficult questions for business families. Too much reliance on the consultants lessens family opportunities to grow together. Too little risks struggles needed to complete the process and to incorporate the experience of others. When possible, it may be helpful to ask the consultant to be accountable to the business's independent board to help balance this issue.

Timing

There is no set timeline for how long it typically takes for a family to develop its Family Agreement. While every experience is unique, some common traits can be identified.

The initiation phase can be incubated for a long time and sometimes can be triggered by unexpected events. The formulation phase generally requires no less than six to eight months. The implementation activities that complete the agreement are mostly concentrated in the year or two after signing.

Conclusion

The process of drafting a Family Agreement is the essence of the agreement's success. A well-designed process grows trust, sharpens communication and decision-making skills, offers practice fields for conflict management, deepens family member relationships and builds family commitment to business continuity.

The process is also, by itself, a catalyst. It sparks attention to succession planning; it brings family together; it opens all the questions to examine governance structures.

Different families will write different values, different policies and different contracts. Success is more a function of the quality of the development process than of the specific nature of the agreement.

VI: Types of Family Agreements

This chapter provides an in-depth examination of the different types of family agreements:

- Family Statement

- Family Business Protocol

- Owners' Contract

- Family Constitution

The Family Statement

The Family Statement primarily focuses on the family as a family. It is philosophical in nature — its core contents are family values and beliefs and may include family business principles. Enforcement comes from moral responsibility. In general, values and principles cover most facets of the family–firm relationship. Sometimes action plans are also mentioned in the text, for example, a statement that principles will be developed into policies later as part of the process of more fully developing the Family Agreement. Here is an outline of a typical Family Statement.

EXHIBIT 19 ■■■■■■■■■■■■■■■■■■■■■■■■■■■■■■■■■■■■■■

The Table of Contents of a Family's Agreement

a. Introduction

b. Our guiding beliefs of the agreement: the values to be transmitted

c. The type of family business we want to be

d. What we expect from our family business

e. Conditions that would lead us to cease to be a family business

f. Principles relating to working in the family business

g. Principles relating to ownership of the family business

h. Principles relating to governing the family business

Consistent with the purpose and contents of the agreement, the process is mostly family oriented. All family members "of age" should be involved, regardless of ownership or employment status. This wide involvement is sought in formulation, approval and implementation. Larger families appoint a task force, as described in Chapter 5, which usually is composed of family members with different roles relative to the business. For instance, executives and future shareholders not working in the business would both be included. Some families consciously include multiple generations and in-laws. The process is generally designed and conducted in a very participative and consensus-oriented way. A family business consultant with a generalist background may be chosen to assist with the whole effort.

The process of developing a Family Statement offers a business-owning family a number of opportunities to enhance its strengths, including these:

- Focusing on family values and beliefs helps the family concentrate its effort on fundamental issues, notably on the reasons why the family wants to remain united.

- Focusing on family business principles helps the family give priority to its most critical decisions, leaving work that is more detailed to the implementation phase.

- The development process facilitates involvement and education of more family members, particularly of those who are young or not employed in the family business.

- Building reliance on values and principles helps resolve family conflict and increases flexibility in dealing with family issues.

Of course, the Family Statement development process also exposes the family to certain risks:

- If a Family Statement is too generic or abstract, it may be difficult for a family to commit to it.

- The effort to achieve agreement on a Family Statement might lead to avoidance of family conflict, leaving conflict unresolved and a danger to genuine commitment.

- The company's non-family executives may not take the Family Statement seriously.

Given these strengths and risks, this type of Family Agreement is particularly suitable to business-owning families who feature close family relations, a strong culture of responsible ownership, a high commitment to the company's continuity and a low level of complexity.

The Family Business Protocol

The Family Business Protocol formally defines family interaction with the business. It is more business focused than the Family Statement. The Family Business Protocol is a normative agreement composed mainly of policies that address the various topics related to the company's needs. It typically addresses issues such as family employment and career development,

The Family Business Protocol is a normative agreement composed mainly of policies that address the various topics related to the company's needs.

systems to regulate how family members are treated in the business, family business governance and management structures and the family members' code of conduct. A protocol should also detail the specific procedures to implement the policies. For example, how a board of directors oversees a family member's performance and compensation might be specified. The document may also deal with how to prepare the family for business governance and management.

Here are outlines of two different Family Business Protocols; one is more comprehensive while the other focuses mostly on family employment.

EXHIBIT 20

Outline of One Family Business Protocol

a. Introduction

b. Goals of the family protocol

c. Object of the family protocol

d. Who signs the family protocol

e. Basic principles of family-firm relationships

f. Ownership structure

g. Group governance: shareholders' meetings and boards

h. Family members' entry into the company

i. The role of managing director and non-executive Chairman

j. Compensation systems for family members

k. Exit from employment for family members

l. Use of company resources by family members

m. Sanctions

n. Protocol's validity

o. Other clauses

Outine of Contents of Another Family's Business Protocol: Fourth Generation Entry Policies and a Self-Regulation

a. Shared general principles

b. Minimum prerequisites for entry

c. Attribution of decision-making power on entry

d. Professional paths for the fourth generation

e. Other opportunities for the fourth generation

f. Preparation for fourth generation ownership role

g. Part-time opportunities

h. Participation of in-laws

As with most Family Business Protocols, these build on already existing Family Statements, referring to values and principles already laid out in previously developed documents.

At an extreme, protocols may be composed only of policies. This might happen when there is no question on shared principles and values (perhaps because a Family Statement already exists), when it is urgent to define some essential rules quickly or when the family does not have the emotional energy for developing family values and mission.

When family members focus only on policies, they risk not achieving a family consensus on values. As discussed in Chapter 4, some Family Business Protocols have been signed with difficulty or even have been postponed because family members realized during the process that their guiding values and principles diverged.

The outline of the first Family Business Protocol (Exhibit 20) also includes two sections for sanctions and clauses, which gives the agreement a contractual flavor and greater emphasis on enforcement. On the other hand, the second protocol does not feature such formality.

In general, families look for legal enforcement to regulate ownership and governance topics. Protocols are typically moral agreements, while ownership poli-

Protocols are typically moral agreements. cies are developed as legally binding contracts or incorporated into the company's bylaws for maximum enforcement.

The process of developing Family Business Protocols can be similar to that for Family Statements. A distinctive feature is that, given the business focus, family members involved are usually those involved in business management and ownership. In addition, advisors and technical experts have a larger role to play in the formulation and implementation of the policies and procedures.

Family Business Protocols feature the following positive aspects:

- They make values and principles concrete.

- They may be more comprehensive. The linkage from value to principle to policy can be shown clearly.

- Formulation may be faster.

- Critical issues can be addressed first.

Less positive aspects also exist.

- There is a risk of underestimating the importance of sharing values and principles.

- Extensive work on policies feels more unfriendly, and mediation may be needed.

- Too much detailing of policies might make the family–firm relation too rigid.

Family Business Protocols are especially suitable for those cases where the same people own and work in the business. Protocols could also fit situations where family and ownership are or will become very complex (as in the second example in Exhibit 20) and there is a specific issue such as employment in the business to regulate quickly.

The Owners' Contract or Shareholders' Agreement

Often called the Shareholders' Agreement, the Owners' Contract is meant to protect the rights of owners. It specifies the legal and contractual understandings among shareholders on ownership and governance issues. Its core content consists, by definition, of ownership and governance policies. All policies are normative and legally enforced in two ways.

Other ownership policies may be included with less legal formality in the Owners' Contract. These policies might include the requirements expected to qualify as a family director or the information shareholders should receive from the company. These policies are usually expressed as guidelines to the board or its nominating committee.

51

EXHIBIT 21

Table of Contents of a Family Owners' Contract

1. Object of the agreement

2. Who signs the agreement

3. Pre-emption and option rights

4. Valuation criteria for buy-sell agreement

5. Dividend rights

6. Shareholders' meetings

7. The board of directors

Sometimes, this type of agreement is stipulated by a subset of family owners, the controlling shareholders. In this case, the minority shareholders may need to consent or not, depending on the laws of the country.

Given the nature of an Owners' Contract, its development process is ownership driven. Consequently, only family shareholders are generally involved in formulation, approval and amendments. All phases are quite formal and are usually assisted by one or more technical experts in juridical and fiscal subjects. Family business consultants are frequently involved to help the family shareholders be clear on their objectives before the agreement is formalized by lawyers.

Owners' Contracts create legal commitments protected by law, assuring shareholders' rights beyond the assurances of less formal family documents. The company's management usually appreciates the shareholders' resolve to protect the company from ambiguity or misunderstanding.

On the other hand, Owners' Contracts lull family members into a false sense of security. Once the Shareholders' Agreement is in place, the family loses the motivation to address other family and business issues, failing to recognize that Owners' Contracts are the "coldest" form of family agreements. The Shareholders' Agreement may guard against certain situations, but it is not sufficient to assure family owners' unity and commitment.

The Family Constitution

The types of Family Agreements we have examined so far take a special perspective — either the family, the business or the ownership point of view. Eventually the business-owning family may become too focused in its orientation to master the

The Family Constitution may articulate the governance practices and family policies for all of the family's institutions.

other dimensions of continuing success. Overemphasis on ownership may alienate the branches of family with little or no ownership. Overemphasis on family can lead to abuses of the business, to preserve family harmony. Overemphasis on the business can offend family — especially family shareholders — not in the business.

Eventually, successful business-owning families focus on all three aspects. They attempt to clarify the interests and needs of family, management and owners. When they do so, they integrate all three types of Family Agreement into a comprehensive document — the Family Constitution.

In larger, more complex business-owning families, the Family Constitution may articulate the governance practices and family policies for all of the family's institutions — family foundation, family office, family investment company, as well as the family businesses. The Family Constitution may also specify the role and procedures of the family council and family meetings.

Generally, a Family Constitution has the following features:

- It serves multiple purposes — giving guidance to the family, the business and ownership.

- It regulates all the family's institutions, not just the business.

- It integrates all the previous discussed Family Agreement types: the Family Statement, the Family Business Protocol and the Owners' Contract.

- It seeks to provide balance when synthesizing all aspects of the Family Agreement.

- It contains both moral and legal enforcement processes.

- Its formulation process is often extremely complex, with different family members participating in different meetings and discussions, depending on their roles in the family, the business and ownership.

- It involves multiple advisors from several disciplines.

EXHIBIT 22 ▰▰▰▰▰▰▰▰▰▰▰▰▰▰▰▰▰▰▰▰▰▰

Sample Family Constitution: List of Documents Included

1. Governance of family and its business (introduction, family aspirations, values, codes of behavior)

2. The group's guiding principles (mission, vision, goals, strategy, ownership, shareholders' meetings, governance bodies, organizational structure, personnel policy, CEO succession)

A framework for next twenty five years (family change, company strengths and weaknesses, strategy guidelines, possible ownership and business scenarios)

4. General principles for strategic plans (values, philosophy, goals)

5. Policies (board design, dividends, liquidity, conflict regulation, company relations with family)

6. The family and the business : general principles for coordination

7. The family office policies

8. Ownership rights and responsibilities

9. Shareholder's Agreement

Advantages of developing a comprehensive Family Constitution include these:

- Integrating the family's and the business's interests.

- Providing a valuable road map for future generations.

- Developing more fully the family council and family governance.

- Allowing different family members to participate and contribute in the formulation process, enhancing their feelings of being involved and considered.

The Family Constitution's main weakness is complexity. There is so much to decide. The risk is that endless formulation efforts may reduce family commitment. If the process becomes overly demanding in terms of time or emotional energy, family members may burn out or give up the process. On the other hand, developing the Family Constitution too quickly risks inadequate appreciation for the benefits of the process. Usually, it is best to formulate the Family Constitution piece-by-piece beginning with topics considered most important, to avoid family members becoming overwhelmed. A review of the four basic types of Family Agreements follows:

EXHIBIT 23 ▐▬▬▬▬▬▬▬▬▬▬▬▬▬▬▬▬

Types of Family Agreements

Distinctive features	Family Statement	Family Business Protocol	Owners' Contract/ Shareholders' Agreement	Family Constitution
Purposes	Focus on Family	Focus on the Family Business	Focus on Ownership	Focus on Family, Ownership and the Business
Character	Philosophical with Moral Enforcement	Normative with Moral Enforcement	Normative with Legal Enforcement	Normative and Philosophical; Moral & Legal Enforcement
Main contents	Family Values and Beliefs Family Business Principles	Family Business Policies and Procedures Expression of Family Commitment to Business Continuity	Family Business Rules on Ownership and Governance Contractual clauses	Family Values and Beliefs Family Business Principles Family Business Policies and Procedures Contractual Clauses
Potential contents	"Action plans"	Family Business Principles under-scoring Policies	Other Family Business Policies put into legal contract	Agreements on other family institutions
Process	Wide involvement of all family members Participative Advisor with general family business background – mostly facilitating	Primarily family members involved in the business (at present or in the future) Participative Advisor with general family business background – facilitating and also providing technical advice and support. Legal and financial experts may also become involved	Only owners involved Formal Technical advisors and family business consultants to clarify goals and objectives as well as facilitation and technical advice	Generally wide involvement of family members; different groups may participate to develop different sections Participative Composite team of advisors: family business and strategy consultants and technicians for legal and financial topics and advisors in other areas of family involvement

Opportunities/ Strengths	Focus on fundamental issues and core decisions Opportunity for family education and involvement	Concrete Concentrated project Efficient Implementation steps clear	Clarity of owners' rights and responsibilities Confidence for business employees Legally defendable	Complete and comprehensive Deep Opportunity for family, ownership and business integrated planning
Risks/ Weaknesses	Too generic and abstract Superficiality	Neglect values and principles Not easily enforceable Rigidity	Less commitment, too much formality Not enough for family ownership unity and commitment to business continuity	Complexity: too much to decide and to be kept alive

VII: Successful Conditions for Developing Family Agreements

Chapters 3 through 6 explored Family Agreements in terms of purposes, contents, process and types. This chapter goes deeper into understanding how family agreements succeed or fail.

Measuring Success

Family business experts generally focus on successful Family Agreements because they are examples of best practice. However, unsuccessful agreements exist as well. What defines a successful or unsuccessful Family Agreement?

Perhaps the most obvious indicator is completion. The Family Agreement has to be signed by all parties involved, or at least by a large majority. Some agreements are abandoned before completion.

Having a signed agreement, however, does not ensure its success. A completed document might feature inappropriate contents, potentially dangerous to the family or the company. Therefore, a second indicator is the quality of the content. Successful agreements contain "good" value statements, principles and/or policies, which respect family business best practices, are internally consistent (see Chapter 4) and are faithful to the agreement's purposes.

Even if the document has perfect contents, however, success is still not ensured. The third and most decisive indicator is whether the agreement impacts behaviour, makes a difference and acts as a catalyst for change. An agreement is successful when values, principles and policies are actually realized. Are the document's intentions realized in action? Does the agreement serve when challenged or when circumstances require amendment?

As described in Chapter 1, Family Agreements are much more than sheets of paper; they are "paper in action" that acts as catalysts for innovation in the family business system. It is almost impossible to appreciate this by just reading the final document. It is important to go behind the contents to see if essential changes have occurred in the family, in ownership or in the company.

Changes sparked by the Family Agreement can be specific and structural. A new Shareholders' Agreement can be written. New family structures such as a family council, foundation or family office may be developed. New ownership structures and governance structures such as holding companies, official shareholders' meetings or an independent board of directors may be formed. Ownership can change by share transfer to the next generation, exit by some owners or other methods. Changes in the company may include implementation of executive committees, new organizational charts, management systems or human resource development programs. New company strategies may be developed. Leadership succession may be catalyzed. New family policies regarding owners' training, liquidity, solidarity, philanthropy or many other topics may be developed.

Less obvious (but also important) effects can result in changes in attitudes and skills. These also reflect on the success of a Family Agreement.

At the company level, examples might include new understandings of roles in the business, strengthened skills or stronger unity and trust within the leadership team.

The three ultimate goals of agreements: they help the company development, they foster ownership unity and commitment and they strengthen the family.

At the ownership level, examples might include stronger awareness of owners' rights and duties, better knowledge of the company, acknowledgment of other owning families' experiences, stronger trust and better communication among the owners, better problem-solving skills as a shareholders' group or the ability to solve conflicts.

At the family level, examples include knowing each other better, learning to constructively confront diverging opinions, improved communication, deeper understanding of the family's and the company's role, strengthened commitment to the company and greater self-confidence as a family.

Clearly, the more obvious structural changes or the less obvious changes in attitude or skills may complement one another to accomplish the three ultimate goals of agreements: they help the company development, they foster ownership unity and commitment and they strengthen the family.

The indicators and measures of a Family Agreement's success analyzed so far are summarized in the following table:

EXHIBIT 24

Assessing a Family Agreement's Success

Completion	✓ Signed
Content quality	✓ Respect of family business "best practices"
	✓ Consistency amongst different contents
	✓ Faithfulness to the Agreement's purposes and principles
Implementation	✓ Consistency between intended and realized actions
	✓ Capacity for renewal:
	• at the time the Agreement is signed and
	• afterwards, by means of proper amendment systems

58

Impact	✓	Structural changes:

            ✓   Structural changes:

- complementary regulations
- new family structures
- new ownership structures
- changes in ownership
- new company structures
- new company strategies
- moves towards succession
- new family strategies

✓   Personal attitude and skill changes:

- better knowledge of one another, of one's company, of other companies and families
- new awareness of family business rights, duties, roles
- better decision-making skills
- more effective communication
- higher trust
- learning how to solve conflicts

Lack of Success

On the other hand, a Family Agreement is unsuccessful if it is not completed or signed, if its contents are ill considered, if it is not applied consistently throughout the family or if hoped-for positive actions do not result.

Unsuccessful Family Agreements may cause damage. The family business is weakened as the new structures the business needs to cope with during its next stages of development are left unrealized. Potentially more serious, the impact of the agreement's failure can undermine personal and business relations. If the family made the effort to formulate the agreement and then it is not implemented, trust in those who had been entrusted with implementation evaporates. Then the company executives take responsibility to execute the agreement away from the family, sometimes losing respect in the family as owners.

The worst result of an unimplemented Family Agreement, however, is that the family becomes cynical and hardened about its capacity to grow, change and perform. When such a spirit is broken, family optimism and willingness to work together to achieve shared goals is extremely difficult to recapture.

Preventing Failure: The Basic Factors

There are usually three sources responsible for the failure of a Family Agreement:

- An attempt to begin development of a Family Agreement when the family is too fragile for candor and interpersonal confrontation.

- Conflicting and hidden motivations for seeking a Family Agreement.

- Inadequate processes for forging the Family Agreement.

Too Fragile a Family. As previously mentioned, Family Agreements are not recommended to replace family therapy, counseling or legal arbitration when those are strongly needed. Deep family differences cannot be glossed over by the hopes of a Family Agreement. The family must have a basic foundation of goodwill, mutual respect and respect for the business itself with its many stakeholders and needs.

The family members included in the process of developing the Family Agreement must be comfortable in the same room together. They must have the basic skills to communicate differences constructively. They must be able to be honest with their personal interests and aspirations.

Where these basics are lacking, a Family Agreement is still possible — after some important groundwork. Family member motivations must be understood, as will be addressed. Those not interested in participating should be excused, with as little judgment and retribution as possible (more times than not, once the process is underway, those not initially interested return to the process.) Most important, where family strength and personal skills are not sufficiently present, the time to address the skills and interpersonal relations should be invested. For some families, this will take time — and will be the best investment the family makes.

To be sure, the family does not have to be expert at interpersonal skills. However, they must understand the basics of the skills so that they can improve through the family meeting process.

Unaligned and Hidden Motivations. Occasionally, Family Agreements are sought for Machiavellian reasons: someone seeks to create a forum to gain control of the business or to create an opportunity to sell their ownership. Perhaps someone wants to create legal rules quickly to protect the business, in their view, from owners' influence or involvement. Such motives may lead to an agreement created under false pretenses and doomed to fail.

If there is any doubt about family member intentions, the Family Agreement process should begin by using

Family Agreements are not recommended to replace family therapy, counseling or legal arbitration.

an advisor or a family business consultant trusted by everyone in the family, to explore the personal interests of each individual. The process can begin if there is a strong, sincere commitment to family unity and business ownership continuity. However, if some family members have the desire to exit ownership or have a conditional commitment to ownership, those wishes can surface and be integrated into the development process. Possible business exits then can be accommodated while family harmony can be solidified.

Poor Process. Most unsuccessful Family Agreements fail not for lack of skills or for the above-mentioned motivations, but for more innocent reasons of poor process. If there is one overriding piece of advice to a family beginning to develop a Family Agreement, it is to pay sincere attention to the process. As urged in Chapter 5, the process is usually more important than the content.

Common Process Mistakes

- Too business driven

- Lack of reflection

- Too much time

- Weak support for family or family business leader

- Abdicated leadership

Process most often goes astray when the family business's leader drives the process in a very directive, top-down manner. Family members then sense that the agreement is to protect the business rather than to strengthen the family. Further, some family members will likely feel that the hard-driving business style of process leadership is uncomfortable or inappropriate in a family setting. Even if all the direct descendants of the owning family are in the business, such an approach can raise anxiety among some of their spouses.

Sometimes the process lacks time for reflection, digestion and comfort. When the process moves too fast, family members have little opportunity to feel ownership for its results and sometimes may feel that the rush violates a sense of fairness. They may ask, "Why go so fast? Is someone trying to do something we don't understand?"

Experience with successful processes suggests that each meeting should review and reaffirm or revise the previous meeting's conclusions before they are voted upon or endorsed. The process may take two to three years to complete a full Family Constitution. On the other hand, the process should not drag on too long, or there is risk of losing the family's commitment to complete the process.

If a strong business-oriented process leader has drawbacks, so, too, does a leader who has limited respect as a leader in the family or limited respect by the family's business leadership. It is not rare that a person in the family, who has never shown much leadership or initiative before, is drawn to the idea of developing a Family Agreement for the family. If that person lacks leadership respect in the family, he or she is best advised to team up with others in the family to initiate the process. The family's business leaders must believe that the family process leadership has regard for and understanding of the business and its requirements for success.

Sometimes there is broad family support for having a Family Agreement, but the family, for reasons of expediency or discomfort, abdicates the leadership of the process to an outside advisor. The family may reason, "The advisor or consultant has done this often and knows best practices. Let her or him draft it for us to review." **This approach is rarely successful.** Every family should use the formulation of its Family Agreement to articulate and clarify its distinct values, to strengthen its decision-making and communications skills and to nurture future family leadership.

One of the most complex challenges facing most business-owning families is how to agree to make its decisions before a decision-making process has been established. As discussed in Chapter 5, the earlier in the process the family can define its decision-making criteria (i.e., consensus or super-majority) the better. The process can be seriously derailed if a very controversial issue arises before a decision-making process is in place. Sometimes in politically charged, branch-oriented families, this becomes a delicate and overriding topic. If so, it is sometimes wise to focus on the non-controversial issues while clearly responding to this open, difficult topic.

Another problem can arise when, despite the process going seemingly well, attendance at meetings begins to decline. Since attendance is voluntary, not everyone feels obliged to participate. While the process may still result in a signed agreement, there could come a time when some might say, "Oh, we didn't understand it that way…" Possibly more troublesome is that those working hard on the process may not feel valued by the family for the effort and contribution they have made.

Conclusion

This chapter focuses on the factors that contribute to the success or failure of the Family Agreement. The challenges are given particular emphasis because many business-owning families have recently discovered the concept and value of Family Agreements. Many advisors advocate developing Family Agreements. Some families pursue a Family Agreement eagerly but lack a full appreciation for the process or a complete understanding of the nature of Family Agreements.

To summarize the ingredients of success in a different way, consider the following "Seven Ps of Highly Effective Family Agreements."

EXHIBIT 25

The Seven P's of Highly Effective Family Agreements

Highly Effective Family Agreements Are

- **Positive:** Family Agreements should emphasize the common good, that the Agreement helps both the family and the business.

- **Philosophical:** Family Agreements should be driven by values and principles, focusing on the owning family's reasons for progressing as family and as business owners.

- **Personal:** Family Agreements should reflect the specific nature, goals and values of the family creating it.

- **Participative:** Family owners should be involved broadly and actively in the process of developing their Family Agreement.

- **Professional:** Never forget that family, business and ownership have inner functioning logics that must be respected.

- **Process & Project oriented:** Family Agreements should recognize the importance of both the process used to create it and the outcome ultimately pursued.

- **Paradoxical resolutions:** Family Agreements should seek creative solutions rather than quickly compromising in the effort to serve simultaneously the business's needs and the family's interests.

Afterword

A Family Agreement, especially a Family Constitution, is the fundamental means and the expression of purpose for the continuity of the business-owning family. A Family Agreement forged in a climate of family goodwill and respect for the special character of a family business promises the opportunity to strengthen the family for generations to come. Paradoxically, this strength comes from the family's commitment to excellence in business ownership. The family concludes that ensuring ownership and company strength also helps ensure family strength. At the same time, a well-governed, united and committed family offers great strength to the business.

The Family Agreement articulates the family's philosophy and outlines the governance procedures to make that philosophy real in practice. **The process itself of developing the Family Agreement can be even more valuable both to family and to business strength.**

The Family Agreement, even in the form of a comprehensive Family Constitution, can never anticipate every question, dilemma, problem or challenge a family will face. Thus, the family's skills in problem solving and decision-making and the family's idealism for family continuity become the cores of long-lasting success. A well-designed and well-implemented *process* for developing and keeping the Family Agreement alive helps the family obtain the strength to overcome new problems and unexpected family circumstances.

> *A Family Constitution synthesizes the family's hopes, the owners' needs and the business's requirements.*

Families often begin the process with either a values-intense Family Statement or a business-focused Family Business Protocol. Families may also begin by reviewing and revising the existing Owners' Contract, first written at the business's founding. As a family collectively considers its future, it may fully develop an integrated Family Constitution. A Family Constitution synthesizes the family's hopes, the owners' needs and the business's requirements. The wonderful result can be family strength, ownership unity and commitment, and business success.

Appendix I

Family Philosophy Statement Example

We trace our roots back seven generations to 1793, when our land-owning ancestors took a spiritual vow to grow a family that contributed to their community. They saw the responsible use and stewardship of that property as a resource to that community, and they gave their children and those that followed the example of conscientious study and breadth of learning. Most of all, they showed a devotion to family and a respect for their heritage.

The thirteen adult family members of these times, by signature below, reaffirm that vow, and pledge to each other mutual support in achieving property stewardship, contribution to society, and personal growth. We seek to pass these values, inspired and nurtured by our ancestors, to our children and to inspire and nurture our children for their children.

Every four months we will all attempt to come together to celebrate these values and to enjoy each other's company.

Appendix II

Owners' Contract

<u>**Outline**</u>

  I. Share Ownership
     A. Eligibility
        1. Descendancy
        2. Gender
        3. Participation in business
        4. Minimum ownership position
        5. Responsibilities
     B. Form
        1. Direct
        2. Trustees or Custodians
        3. Voting Rights

  II. Share Transfer
     A. Distribution
        1. Eligibility
        2. Notification
     B. Redemptions
        1. Conditions
        2. Amounts
        3. Valuation
        4. Teams
        5. Priorities
        6. Funding

Appendix III

Family Business Protocol

<u>Headlines</u>

1.0 Purpose

To maintain and continue the family company.

2.0 Philosophy

    2.1   This agreement is intended to conserve and perpetuate the wealth created by the founders.

    2.2   The agreement seeks to avoid the traps common to families in business.

        2.2.1 To avoid incompetent family management.

        2.2.2 To assure that market conditions drive business decisions, not family needs.

        2.2.3 To provide adequate capital for the business to protect and extend its competitive position.

        2.2.4 To clarify the rules of succession.

    2.3   This agreement carries the full authority of "family law."

    2.4   This agreement covers the topics of ownership, direction, participation and conduct.

3.0 Parties

The members of the family that incorporate this agreement are all the shareholders of record on the date of this agreement, as undersigned.

4.0 History

    4.1   The family company was founded in 1957 by a member of a family with trading origins dating back more than 100 years.

    4.2   The Company was founded as a wholesale distributor of food products. That remained its primary business until 1991.

    4.3   In 1991 the Company began a series of acquisitions in the retail and real estate businesses. These three sectors – wholesale food, retail, and commercial property development and management – are now, and for the near future, the core areas of the business.

    4.4   The male children of the founders all joined the business and now hold executive positions.

    4.5   The founders initiated this protocol to keep the company in the family for another generation.

5.0 Assumed Obligations

    5.1 The signatories to this agreement have willingly committed to the expectations in the protocol.

    5.2 The signatories shall obey all the regulations and norms of the agreement.

    5.3 The signatories shall augment this agreement with other policies as determined necessary to fulfill its purpose.

    5.4 The signatories agree to review and affirm this document every two years at the Shareholders' Assembly.

    5.5 The signatories commit to communicate and assure the agreement for the next generation.

6.0 Termination

    6.1 This agreement is terminated upon the sale of the Company.

    6.2 It is also terminated on two-thirds majority of the shares.

    6.3 Fifty-one percent of the shares may terminate this agreement and/or sell the company with two-thirds consent of the Board of Directors if, in the determination of the board, the family is not fulfilling its responsibilities to the Company.

7.0 Ownership

    7.1 Ownership shall be exclusive to direct descendants or legally adopted heirs of the founders.

    7.2 The family company shall remain exclusively owned by family members.

        7.2.1 Subsidiaries may include equity partners, so long as the Family Company holds 50% of the subsidiary voting shares.

        7.2.2 Non-family management may participate in phantom ownership opportunities.

    7.3 All family members are expected to follow the shareholders' agreement and to sign prenuptial agreements in advance of marriage.

        7.3.1 The Company shall provide legal counsel to assist any shareholder in their ownership continuity planning.

        7.3.2 Each shareholder shall share their estate plans and share owning continuity plans as pertains to company shares with the Company's general counsel and the president of the family office.

        7.3.3 All adult shareholders are expected to attend the Annual Shareholders' Assembly.

        7.3.4 Shareholders are expected to refrain from any investments or activity that would benefit a company competitor. Each shareholder should report any possible conflicts of interest with the Company Chairman who will discuss the report with the Board of Directors.

8.0 Liquidity

    8.1 The Company's Shareholders Agreement specifies share redemption rights.

        8.1.1 The Company will provide a written, certified valuation of Company shares, in accordance with the shareholder buy-sell agreement, to each shareholder within 60 days after the end of the fiscal year.

        8.1.2 The Company will disclose to all shareholders any redemption by the Company or transactions among the shareholders.

    8.2 The Company will arrange a Company guaranteed line of credit to provide shareholder loans up to 50% of the value of their shares.

    8.3 The Company's Board of Directors will propose to the shareholders at each annual Shareholders' Assembly a dividend policy expected at least to maintain an average dividend payout of 15% of net operating income.

9.0 Family Member Employment

    9.1 All descendants of the founders and their spouses and relatives of their spouses are subject to this policy.

    9.2 From this date forward, all family 23 or older seeking employment, full or part time, shall meet the following conditions:

        9.2.1 Bachelor's degree or equivalent from an accredited university.

        9.2.2 Minimum of three years full time employment at another organization.

        9.2.3 Able to conduct business in English.

        9.2.4 A graduate degree in business or science is encouraged.

    9.3 All family 16-23 years of age are welcome and encouraged to work in the company part time or summers during their school years.

    9.4 Both members of a married couple may not be employed in the Company.

    9.5 The Company will strive, as best as is possible, to avoid siblings from reporting directly to each other or their parent.

    9.6 The Company will provide at Company cost reasonable career counseling to all family members.

    9.7 All family employees shall be subject to Company retirement policies or not to exceed 70 years of age, whichever is younger.

9.8　A committee of independent directors on the Company board will review and approve all employment arrangements, compensation and expense accounts of family members.

10.0　Board of Directors

10.1　The Board of Directors of the holding company shall be comprised of at least three independent directors.

10.2　Independent directors shall serve a maximum of ten years.

10.3　Family shareholders are welcome to attend and observe board meetings – except the executive sessions of the independent directors – with permission of the Chairman of the Board. No more than two observers shall attend any meeting.

10.4　The board of the Company shall conduct self-assessment each year that includes a confidential survey of all family shareholders.

10.5　The Board of Directors will elect its Chairman.

10.5.1 It is preferred that the Chairman be a family shareholder.

10.5.2 It is preferred that the Chairman not be an employee of the Company.

10.6　Director positions will be nominated annually in accordance with Company bylaws, by the board Nominating Committee that shall be composed of 50% of family shareholders who do not serve on the board or work in the Company.

11.0　Shareholder Communications

11.1　The Company will hold an Annual Shareholders' Assembly, in accordance with the Company bylaws, and pay all reasonable travel costs of family shareholders.

11.2　All shareholders shall make all inquiries for information or suggestions to the Company through the Chairman of the Board.

11.3　The Shareholders, at their Annual Assembly, shall affirm or modify the Company's three-year goals for growth and profit and market value and charitable giving and the Company's capital structure.

12.0　Amendments

12.1　The provisions of this protocol may be revised by an affirmative vote of two-thirds of voting shareholders.

12.2　Every three years the independent directors of the board will provide all shareholders with their assessment of the appropriateness of the conditions of this protocol.

Notes & Suggested Readings

Foreword

2002 American Family Business Survey, Raymond Institute, Alfred, New York, 2002.

Chapter 2

Strategic Planning for the Family Business: Parallel Planning to Unify the Family and Business by Randel S. Carlock, Ph.D. and John L. Ward, Ph.D. (Palgrave, 2001).

Chapter 4

Developing Family Business Policies: Your Guide to the Future by Craig E. Aronoff, Ph.D., Joseph H. Astrachan, Ph.D. and John L. Ward, Ph.D. (Family Enterprise Publishers, 1998).

"The Role of Family in Family Business," by Guido Corbetta and Daniela Montemerlo (editors), special issue of *Family Business Review* (n. 3, 2002).

"Valores corporativos y empresas familiares," by Guido Corbetta, in D. Melé Carné (editor) *Consideraciones éticas sobre la iniciativa emprendedora y la empresa familiar,* (EUNSA, Navarra, 1999).

Chapter 5

Family Meetings: How to Build a Stronger Family and a Stronger Business by Craig E. Aronoff, Ph.D. and John L. Ward, Ph.D. (Family Enterprise Publishers, 2002).

"Family Protocols in Spain: A Survey on 10 Years of Experience," by M. A. Gallo and Salvo Tomaselli, in S. Tomaselli, L. Melin (editors), *Family Firms in the Wind of Change*, (FBN-IFERA, 2004).

Web Sites

AIdAF (Associazione Italiana delle Aziende Familiari): www.aidaf.it

Family Enterprise Publishers: www.efamilybusiness.com

IEF (Instituto de la Empresa Familiar): www.iefamiliar.com

The Authors

Daniela Montemerlo

Daniela Montemerlo, is professor of Business Administration at Bocconi University and senior faculty member of the Strategic and Entrepreneurial Management Department at Bocconi School of Management

She is the author of a book on Family Business Governance and of numerous articles and case studies on family business issues on national and international academic journals and professional magazines.

Since the early '90s she has been founder and director of many family business programs at SDA Bocconi. Since the inception of the Italian Association of Family Firms she has directed its activities and takes part in research, training and lobbying.

As a consultant, she assists small and medium-size family businesses on family protocols, design and management of family & company governance bodies, family and company check-ups, strategic planning, organizational change, successors' training and mentoring. She is independent board member of a fifth-generation Italian family company.

Daniela is partner of the consulting company Impresa Sviluppo and a member of The Family Business Consulting Group International.

Daniela's work in the family business field is internationally acknowledged. She is a board member of the International Family Enterprise Research Academy and has served on the FFI's Advisory Committee from 1998 to 2001. In 2001, she was a co-winner of the FFI International Award.

She earned her university and Doctoral degrees at Bocconi University. She resides in Milano.

John L. Ward, Ph.D.

John L. Ward, Ph.D. is a co-founder of The Family Business Consulting Group, Inc.® and clinical professor at Kellogg School of Management. Ward teaches strategic management, business leadership and family enterprise continuity. He is an active researcher, speaker and consultant on family succession, ownership, governance and philanthropy.

He is the author of many leading texts on family business including, *Keeping the Family Business Healthy, Creating Effective Boards for Private Enterprises, Strategic Planning for the Family Business* and *Perpetuating the Family Business: 50 Lessons Learned from Long-Lasting Successful Families in Business.* He is also co-author of a collection of booklets, *The Family Business Leadership Series*, each focusing on specific issues family businesses face.

Ward graduated from Northwestern University (B.A.) and Stanford Graduate School of Business (M.B.A. and Ph.D.). He is the co-director of The Center for Family Enterprises at Kellogg and currently serves on the boards of several companies in the U.S. and Europe. He conducts regular seminars in Spain, Italy, India, Hong Kong, Sweden, and Switzerland.

Index

77